What is A Patriot?

This word, Patriot, should stir a well of emotions. From The American Revolution to "Love of Country" the thoughts and feelings are strong. Accusations of being *unpatriotic* are thrown around as insults and as attacks against opponents of government (primarily foreign) policy.

> **Patriot** *– Person who vigorously supports their country and is prepared to defend it*[1]

An American discussion of the word "Patriot" must be started by mentioning the American Revolution. A Patriot during that time was one who supported the Declaration of Independence (*"supports their country"*). This was strictly a rejection of the authority of the British Crown. Since the British Crown chose to reverse this Declaration with force, being a Patriot required the acceptance of the use of force (*"is prepared to defend it"*). Being a Patriot and not willing to fight was suicide and thus meaningless. Thomas Paine was the quintessential Patriot author.

> **Patriot** *– One who loves his country, and zealously supports its authority and interests*[2]

For a non-American a Patriot is one who accepts the authority of their country. For a Britain or a colonial Tory during the American Revolution this was the Crown. The recognized authority had been and was expected to be the Crown. This emphasis on the country's authority is strikingly revealing. It is the specific omission of 'authority' in the American definition of "Patriot" which reveals that the Country is the target of a Patriot's support.

> **Authority** *– Legal or rightful power; a right to command or to act; power exercised buy a person in virtue of his office or trust*

Authority resides in a country's government. The idea of America was created before it had its own government. The government was created several years after declaring independence. Thus there were (American) Patriots before there was a recognized government. Throughout history most countries' authority developed after a person became the dominant force in a geographical area. Authority is intentionally not included in the American definition of a Patriot.

> **Nationalist** – *One who advocates national unity and independence*[3]

Contrasted to a Patriot, a Nationalist is slightly but importantly different. Nationalism focuses on the unique characteristics of an ethnically and historically separate group of people. America, being largely created by voluntary immigrants from many, often mutually hostile nations and their offspring, was never really a nation. A Nationalist often adopted blind, non-rational support for their country ("*national unity*") and its accepted authority. A Patriot is not: *advocating the interests of one's own country exclusively, regardless of the effects of a country's actions on other countries*[4]

A Patriot loves and supports its country. It is a love of the country itself. So what is this country called America? The essence of anything is that what makes it unique from all other similar things. The essence of America is the *Declaration of Independence*. Therefore an American Patriot is one who loves this document and what it represents. What made America so unique (in 1776) was:

- "…that all men are created equal, that they are endowed by their Creator with certain unalienable Rights, that among these are Life, Liberty and the pursuit of Happiness…"[1]

Most people today do not understand how so revolutionary this was in 1776. There had been no country for thousands of years – if ever – whose leading members dared write such a statement. This was not only written in America's founding document but essentially defined America.

The target of an American Patriot's support predates the authority of the country. Being an American Patriot does not require one to support the authority (i.e., government) of the country. The first and primary statements in the *Declaration of Independence* referring to government are:

- "...to secure these rights, Governments are instituted among Men, deriving their just powers from the consent of the governed..."[5]
- "...whenever any Form of Government becomes destructive of these ends, it is the Right of the People to alter or to abolish it, and to institute new Government..."[6]

An American Patriot therefore is not required to support the day's government or its policy. Governments, in a republic, come and go. What an American Patriot supports are the transcendent ideas of the country stated most eloquently above. All persons equally enjoy rights and governments are created as a tool to secure these rights. An American Patriot does not love but uses the government.

For an American Patriot "Love of Country" cannot be an acceptance of the principle: my country no matter what. "No matter what" would at least allow and encourage the forfeiting of a country's founding ideas. If these ideas are disconnected from the country then all a Patriot would have to love is perhaps the separate group of people. Love of a country not defined by ideas would no doubt lead to nationalism.

As long as this country holds true to the ideas of "life, liberty, and pursuit of happiness", I will call myself a Patriot.

Gerald Luhman, II
Litchfield, Connecticut
25 May 2005

[1] www.webster-dictionary.org/Patriot
[2] www.askoxford.com
[3] www.webster-dictionary.org/definition/nationalist
[4] www.webster-dictionary.org/definition/nationalism
[5] *Declaration of Independence*
[6] *Declaration of Independence*

<u>Why the Right Wing and Left Wing Love Each Other</u>

Just like a see-saw cannot exist without two opposing ends the generally-assumed political spectrum of right and left cannot exit without both ends. These two sides vie for the goods of political spoils. When Martin Van Buren first formalized the political party, he stated that the purpose of the political party was to provide jobs and the benefit of political party to their allies. There was little difference in the party philosophy. Power and benefits were the goal of the party system.

These two sides vie for power against each other. This fight happens while the remainder of our country seeks only to be left alone.

If you analyze the last two presidential elections, one realizes very few persons are choosing the president. Roughly 50% percent of the eligible electorate actually voted. 50% each chose the two primary candidates. That means only 25% of the elector chose the President. The non-voting 50% had very little interest in which the President was. Does this mean they were apathetic or did they just realize that they were not in the political process to "get jobs" as Martin Van Buren would have argued?

The President **should** have little impact on American lives. In a society of limited government, the federal government should not impact our personal lives. To the extent that they do, it is sad commentary on our polity.

Gerald Luhman, II
Litchfield, Connecticut
29 December 2007

My Flag

This is a simple claim. A piece of cloth in the form of the officially recognized emblem of our country is owned by someone, in this case by me.

The defining feature (the essence) of our country is the Declaration of Independence which concretized the idea of our country and the US Constitution which established the US Government at the behest of the states. The flag is not our country's essence. Flags were originally used as a means of identifying armed forces on a battlefield.

"Flag burning" is defined as a public conflagration of the US flag as a means of *showing off* one's disapproval of the country.

Burning of one's country flag is a partial form of intellectual destruction. Being the only country founded upon an idea(s) and not upon some genetic or ethnic collective, one either agrees or disagrees with the idea of our country. Of course this idea is complex or multifaceted so one does not need to agree with all aspects. However, the essence of our country (see above documents) can be clearly formulated.

If one accepts (or even embraces) this idea, then flag burning can only be an act of idiocy or self-hatred.

Officers authorized by our Constitution are not even bound to defend the flag. They are sworn to defend the Constitution "from all enemies, both foreign and domestic". The Constitution (not to mention the idea of our country) supersedes the flag.

A flag is owned (normally) by an individual. An individual has the right – in this country – to "life liberty, and pursuit of happiness". If I want to self-negate myself (though as a rational being I never would), then I have that right and freedom to do so.

Prohibition of flag burning is both self-contradictory itself and ineffective. It is ineffective as it will not achieve its intended (though rarely mentioned) aim – to instill love of and reduce hate of our country. Love and hate can never be forced upon one by another. Prohibiting of liberty over property in a country founded upon its free exercise is obviously wrong.

Flag burning should not be forbidden.

Gerald Luhman, II
Litchfield, Connecticut
13 January 2008

Reason, Deified

Why would one deify reason?

Here I will not describe reason or reasonableness but simply say that reason is the ability to think that human beings have and other animals do not have. To deify reason is to place it in a position of supreme value, i.e. above all others.

With Reason humans know reality. Reality is the existence of everything and is independent of human thought and action. Reality is perceived with the five senses and Reason is used to "know" what is not immediately sensed. Without sensation, Reason is not possible; without Reason, sensation is less useful.

Only individuals can reason; the capacity to reason is possessed by all individuals. One cannot reason for another though one can show how to reason or help another to reason.

If one does not rely on Reason to "know" reality, then the other believed method of knowing reality is divination. Divination is the supposed receipt of knowledge from another. Divination can be believed to come from a supernatural being or a person of authority. The acceptance of either type of assurance leads one to rely on the thinking of another. This leads to being a follower and not an independent person.

In closing, I will throw out a closing reminder. Reason led us to The Age of Reason and Enlightenment lead to capitalism and republicanism and took us away from divination of monarchy and medieval religion.

Gerald Luhman, II
Litchfield, Connecticut
9 July 2008

Wire Tap the Doctors

This might sound bizarre or even dangerous, but I will outline a situation of political allies that will lead to doctors being wire tapped.

Certain persons in the political landscape think that more freedoms need to be curtailed in order to protect our national security. These persons are conventionally referred to as 'right' or 'right wing'. They focus on the dangers to our freedoms from persons who are intent on destroying our infrastructure.

Other persons in the same landscape think that other freedoms need to be curtailed in order to protect our personal security. These persons are conventionally referred to as 'left' or 'left wing'. They focus on the dangers faced by persons lacking the desire and/or ability to take care of themselves.

However I assert that these are just the opposite side of the same coin. Just as a coin cannot exist without two sides these two security-fearful viewpoints live together.

There is a growing movement for our federal government to nationalize the healthcare industry. There is also a growing movement for the federal government to spy on its citizens. Once the government controls the healthcare, doctors will be government employees.

These doctors might make independent decision out of their own (heaven-forbid) concern for their patients to cut corners or bridge gaps in the healthcare regulations. These intentions are only the welfare of their patients. Faced with bureaucratic regulations sometimes they will have chosen the former over the latter.

In order for the government to control these possible shortcuts, the government will become concerned about doctors' independent decisions. Wiretapping the doctors phones, emails might be started to find those doctors making independent decisions. No bureaucracy likes independent decisions.

Gerald Luhman, II
Litchfield, Connecticut
13 January 2008

All Want Profit

It is true. If you are willing to understand the concept of profit, then I am confident that you will realize that you do seek it. (When I say 'you' I mean everyone who reads this essay and even everyone who is at least a reading and a thinking person.)

Profit is simply the difference in the cost and the revenue of an activity. It is the difference between what comes in and what goes out; the cost and the benefit.

Profit is typically achieved by moral and legal means. I assume everyone acts legally until proven otherwise. For an example, if my son prepares 1 gallon of lemonade from scratch costing $5.00 and selling individually each 6-ounce glass for $0.75, this is profit because 1 gallon = 4 quarts = 8 pints = 16 cups. 16*.75 = $12. This profit is certainly moral for him to keep. He created this 'extra value', this profit. He is not only justified to keep this value; but also obligated to keep it. He created it. It is his creation. It is his…just as much as his own body, his own educated mind, his own athletic strength.

What if my son becomes more successful? Suppose he is selling over 300 cups of lemonade every weekend day. (2 * 300* $0.75 = $450). Other potential suppliers, i.e., other children in the neighborhood) hear about this. They might open their own stand. They should get some praise for having the initiative to do this but not as much as my son.

Not only do businessman or Wall Street professionals seek profit. The so-called "common person" seeks it. Why does she or he go to one store or another? Do you go to the one that higher price for the same item? Are you willing to pay more taxes to your local, state, federal government?

Gerald Luhman, II
Sarasota, Florida
25 May 2012

From an Atheist to all Atheists.

Don't force acceptance. Regardless of being one of the smallest minorities in the US, atheists[1] should not force others to accept us.

"In God We Trust" on the US federal paper currency is insignificant. The paper money is becoming less valuable every year; there is no objective value supporting it. It is backed only by Faith. Thus this phrase on it is quite ironic though sad. Perhaps only trusting in God will keep the money's value stable.

It is more important to understand and teach why the phrase was added to the Federal Reserve note. Just understanding – rather than forcing to remove it – is the proper course of action.

We do not need acceptance. The Constitution and its foundation of natural rights does not give us the right to be accepted. It prohibits Congress from abridging free exercise of religion. Nowhere in the US has the Constitution's First Amendment been significantly violated. (This cannot be said about the following Amendment.) There is little danger of persons being persecuted for their religion or non-religion.

If we force religious persons to accept us, we would be hypocritical by using force and unreasoned assertions to make an ethical point. Only perception and reason, not faith, are the true sources of knowledge. Forcing others to accept us is the equivalent of using faith to make a point. What nonsense for an atheist!

Gerald Luhman, II
Sarasota, Florida
10 April 2013

---

[1]*Atheism is not the denial of God or other supernatural beings but is the non-acceptance of the existence of these.* **(See: en.wikipedia.org. Atheism** is, in a broad sense, the rejection of belief in the existence of deities. In a narrower sense, atheism is specifically the position that there are no deities. Most inclusively, atheism is simply the absence of belief that any deities exist. **Agnosticism** is the view that the existence or non-existence of any deity is unknown and possibly unknowable.)

Do Not Call It Obamacare

Opponents of the recent federal overhaul of the US healthcare industry should **not** call it "Obamacare". The passage of the **Patient Protection and Affordable Care Act (PPACA)** was a long time coming. There are two reasons why we should not refer to by its colloquial name. One is that it is wrong and one that it diverts valid opposition.

Firstly, it was not a result of one man's triumph or (as some would describe) 'ramming it down the throats of Americans'. President Obama simply rode a train of personal and party popularity following two wars. The Democratic Party has been advocating socialized medical care since at least the 1930s. Incrementally they have steadily increased the federal government control over & responsibility for health care: Roosevelt, Johnson, Clinton, and Obama. The greater strides in government control over society are always done at times of leaders' ascending popularity. A public official recently said that a crisis should never be wasted; but real success comes from not wasting the sudden the popularity that a crisis gives. Even the Republican Party greatly increased the federal government's role with the passage of **Medicare Part D.**

Secondly, this focus on one man as the owner/creator/identification of this massive government grab focuses the attention on the wrong thing. Subconsciously this allows too many persons to think that if Obama was not reelected or after Obama leaves office then all will be okay. They will be mistaken. The focus should be on the government's role in our lives and the idea that we are responsible for others. This idea that "we are responsible for another's" health care really means that "you are responsible for my" health care.

If you really oppose this program you can only do it out of one of two principles: 1) that the Federal Government is trampling on States Rights or 2) that the Federal Government is trampling on the Individual Rights. Focus on the encroaching collectivism not the fleeting, temporary figurehead of the movement.

Gerald Luhman, II
Sarasota, Florida
26 August 2013

In the past fourteen years US media has focused attention on American Exceptionalism. I refer to:

American exceptionalism is the theory that the United States is qualitatively different from other nation states.[1]

There are objective facts that prove this "theory" correct. However, it is more important to answer the following questions: What are these differences? Do these differences still existing or have they been overshadowed by other differences?

The United States of America was the first[2] country to be created by a conscious, deliberate, rational, open debate. The debate occurred among **elected** representatives. The end product of this debate, The Declaration of Independence, announced the creation of the country by explaining its reason for becoming, its justification for self-creation and its credo.

A brief review of history will highlight this exceptionalism. From the beginning of written history (and most likely ever since the achievement of agricultural societies) most governments or proto-governments were created by "strong men". Either there was a military conqueror who set up a "government" by force or a family gradually assumed/took over control of an area. Historically, all large political organizations were led by strong-men who often passed on their authority to their offspring (usually sons). Sometimes palace intrigues or different strong men violently usurped the existing ruler. The existence of monarchy was vast, strong and most importantly normal.

The writing and adoption of the Declaration of Independence was the single shining proof of American Exceptionalism. No other country was established with the premise of:

We hold these truths to be self-evident, that all men are created equal, that they are endowed by their Creator with certain unalienable Rights, that among these are Life, Liberty and the pursuit of Happiness.--That to secure these rights, Governments are instituted among Men, deriving their just powers from the consent of the governed,

Not only was this not ever written but it was never the catalyst for a new country.

The retirement of the first (Constitutional) President of these United States solidified this exceptionalism. The fact that George Washington was (in some quarters) requested to become *President for Life* was expected. The fact that there was not enough pressure to start a future monarchy was even more unusual.

The detractors of this view discount this evidence from the standpoint of today's societies. The inclusion of only white males in the political involvement in the Republic was not unusual. Nevertheless at the time this Republic had the greatest suffrage in the world. Without violating common sense, today's standards cannot diminish the exceptionalism of this Republic's birth.

The Republic was a direct outcome of the Age of (European) Enlightenment. The persons that immigrated were seeking freedom with a certain sense of life. The Republic's distance from Europe prevented the negative influence of feudalism still lingering over European at the time.

This openness – again compared to the times – required a limited (federal) government. And a limited government was demanded. This new government was created by another deliberate, rational (though not public) discourse. The federal government was created with limits on its authority. Persons were declared as having rights which the government, either state or federal, could not abridge.

The increasing role of government, internally and externally, over the past 100 years has reduced this exceptionalism. The growing role as a world power/leader – gladly encouraged by some (e.g., T. Roosevelt) and reluctantly pursued by others (e.g., H. Truman) put us on a path of historical normality. Internally the increasing role of the government is obvious today though it has been growing for the past hundred years. The Republic is becoming more like the less open and more rigid societies with government as society's "problem solver".

This Republic is now not so different from other countries, especially those of Europe. The Republic was exceptional in its creation. The Exceptionalism has diminished over time.

Gerald Luhman, II
Bradenton, Florida
13August 2014

---

[1] http://en.wikipedia.org/wiki/American_exceptionalism
[2] There is the possibility that another country was first but there is no written evidence

Escaped Slaves Are Not Illegal Immigrants

I prefer the term "illegal immigrants" rather than "illegal aliens". It is more exact and does not conjure up non-earth creatures.

Today a MSNBC talk show guest compared[1] a female slave of the 1800's who escaped the South to New Hampshire and married a free man to today's illegal immigrants. They indirectly pleaded that we could not make illegal immigrants leave the US because we now know that slavery was bad.

Slavery is always bad; it does not take a 21st Century viewpoint to know that. American slavery was bad because it was in effect Europeans kidnapping or buying Africans from other Africans and bringing them under violence to America to work. Violence was the means by which these persons were kept and were forced to work.

The show guest described both a free man traveling from upper New York State to Washington, D.C. on a business trip and persons violating laws by entering in a national boarder, as "They choose a legitimate form of work." It was legitimate for the free man to travel to another state, but it is not legitimate for persons to illegally cross s borders. Illegal immigration is persons violating the entry laws of a country and remaining illegally in place.

Of course if violence is used to keep an illegal immigrant in place then that would be slavery. However since they were able to steal away from the own country and enter the US without being caught they very likely able to do the reverse.

Gerald Luhman, II
Bradenton, Florida
24 February 2015

---

[1] http://www.truthrevolt.org/news/msnbcs-melissa-harris-perry-illegal-immigration-modern-form-slavery